Free Our Girls

HUMAN TRAFFICKING
AWARENESS, PREVENTION & RESPONSE

A Comprehensive Training Manual

The First in the #BeTheKey Series

WARNING:

Graphic Content

User Discretion is Advised

CONTENTS

OBJECTIVES

The Free Our Girls' *Human Trafficking Awareness, Prevention & Response: A Comprehensive Training Manual* meets the objectives of human trafficking awareness as outlined by the Department of Homeland Security:

- Understand the difference between smuggling, trafficking and prostitution
- Define human trafficking
- Recognize populations vulnerable to human trafficking
- Recognize indicators of human trafficking

The violation of basic human rights that is known as human trafficking. Human trafficking occurs in two forms: labor trafficking and sex trafficking. Human trafficking, in both forms, occurs on every continent, and in every country around the world. Worldwide, it is estimated that approximately 68% of human trafficking is labor trafficking, and 22% is sex trafficking. While accurate data is often difficult to find due to this black market industry's secretive, criminal nature, there are estimates that over 20 million people are trafficked and enslaved through one or both forms worldwide each year. To personalize this number, 1 in every 236 people in the world is trapped in modern slavery, meaning that you are very likely to know someone within your personal social network that is, or has been, exploited through trafficking. Human trafficking is the second largest source of illegal income worldwide, estimated at $150 billion per year, exceeded only by drug trafficking (larger than Google, Amazon and eBay's revenues combined). And while labor trafficking is a larger percentage of trafficked individuals, sex trafficking nets approximately 66% of the profits.

Free Our Girls is focused on awareness, prevention and response to sex trafficking and commercial sexual exploitation. While we will look briefly at labor trafficking, this comprehensive training manual is focused on addressing sex trafficking, and more specifically, what sex trafficking looks like in the United States. It is estimated that at least 14,000 individuals are smuggled into the US each year to be trafficked, 83% of confirmed human trafficking cases here involve American born citizens. When we look at the issue of domestic sex trafficking, it is important to note that while traffickers exploit both males and females, minors and adults, sex trafficking most often affects females (92%), and those who are Black (40%). With females being the overwhelming gender that is victimized through commercial sexual exploitation, approximately 73% are adults, and the 27% that are minors are typically first recruited and exploited between the ages of 11 and 14. And while there are few accurate statistics on the victims of human trafficking, there are even fewer for the traffickers and customers. While data for the suppliers and buyers is in the preliminary gathering stages, we can say with confidence that an overwhelming majority of traffickers and customers are male.

We find it important to note that there are absolutely male victims and female predators, and through our outreach and work we have encountered situations involving every citizenship status, race, and gender, economic and educational background. And while Free Our Girls' focus is educating the community on the males that supply and purchase women and girls for the purpose of commercial sexual exploitation, we do not discriminate against any other trafficking situation.

Sex trafficking is modern day slavery, with the average daily quota women are required to bring their trafficker being between $500 and $1000. Most women work every day of the week, with only a few days off per year – traffickers typically do not allow their victims to take time off when they are sick, injured, or menstruating. Women are expected to work until they meet their daily quota, which can take an average of 10-12 hours, yet they are often forced to stay in hotels and on the streets for 18-24 hours per day. This stressful work environment and unattainable expectations, combined with the social use of drugs, women often turn to illicit substances to manage anxiety, help keep them awake or fall asleep, and to escape the daily exploitation and isolation they experience, and end up developing substance abuse and addiction problems that must be addressed in order to begin working on helping them to find their freedom from slavery. It is said that there are three options for a trafficked woman outside of the one her trafficker provides for her: to escape, be rescued, or die. Poor working and living conditions, lack of ability to seek quality healthcare, substance abuse and violence from both traffickers and buyers greatly affects a prostituted woman's quality of life. In fact, the life expectancy of a trafficked individual, once they enter the world of exploitation, is approximately 7 years. Due to a lack of community awareness and resources, at this time, sadly, only about 1-2% of trafficking victims are ever rescued. It is Free Our Girls' goal to not only see thousands of sexually exploited women and girls find their freedom, but to prevent thousands more from ever falling victim.[1]

---

[1]Statistic Referenced in this Section:
US DHHS, UNODC, International Labor Organization, Polaris Project, US DOJ

AWARENESS

[*uh*-**wair**-nis]

noun

1. the state or condition of being aware; having knowledge; consciousness:

The object of Empathy Week is to raise awareness of how human trafficking affects our community.

AWARENESS

The general idea of what human trafficking is comes from what the media and pop culture tells you it is. You may have a sensationalized picture in our head, like the international kidnapping, drug and prostitution operation in the *Taken* movie series. You may have an the perspective that women involved in prostitution take part willingly; it is either a glamourous lifestyle of luxury and love like in *Pretty Woman*, or disease-ridden and drug-addled like the reality show *Intervention*. Or images of illegal immigrants in shipping containers on east coast docks, like the storylines in *Law & Order SVU,* may come to mind. It is important to know that while human trafficking can contain elements of these Hollywood scenarios, domestic sex trafficking for the most part looks entirely different than this. These pop culture interpretations of what human trafficking are contain elements of smuggling, prostitution *and* human trafficking. They are all exploitative of an individual who has a lack of opportunities. However, there are very distinct differences between these three illegal activities that can help us determine whether or not someone is experiencing commercial sexual exploitation. In fact, according to Human Trafficking Search: The Global Resource & Database, 71% of situations typically involve someone the victim knows and trusts, and unless you know the risk factors and indicators of commercial sexual exploitation are much less easily identified.

KEY POINT: WHEN MAINSTREAM SOCIETY ISN'T SURE ABOUT WHAT HUMAN TRAFFICKING LOOKS LIKE, THEY ARE NOT ABLE TO PREVENT IT, OR HELP VICTIMS.

The easiest way to understand smuggling, human trafficking and prostitution is a Venn diagram, which illustrates the differences, and the overlap of these activities in particular circumstances.

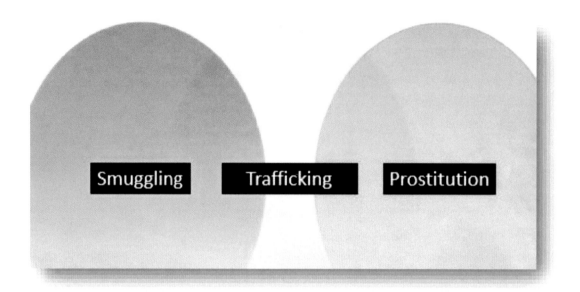

Smuggling is a one-time event that involves transporting an individual across international borders. There is typically a fee that the individual pays their smuggler, and once they have been taken across the border, the transaction is complete and the relationship ends. This scenario is commonly seen as illegal immigration by foot, in car, or in underground tunnels from Canada and Middle and South Americas.

Prostitution is the exchange of sexual services for money, and is illegal here in the United States (except for a few counties in Nevada). Prostitution is one of many activities that fall under the larger category of sex work, which includes adult films, nude webcam modeling, "happy ending" massage parlors, street and online prostitution, phone sex hotlines, and escort services. There is a thin line between legal and illegal sex work here in the United States, and often the legal forms of sex work are a front for the illegal. For example, online prostitution is advertised as escort work, which is legal here in the US, as it is compensation for time and companionship, not sexual services. However, a majority of the time prostitution is what occurs behind closed doors.

Understand that prostitution itself is not automatically human trafficking. There are individuals that willingly take part in prostitution as their choice of employment. The Justice Department partnered with the Urban Institute for a survey of prostituted individuals in the US, and their data indicated that there are approximately 1 million adult female prostitutes in the United States. Sadly, 90% of the women interviewed by WHISPER Oral History Project indicated that they had been under the control of a pimp or trafficker. A common belief here in America is that prostitutes are "legally consenting adults," and while they do exist, it is likely that far more are not there by choice.

Human Trafficking includes labor trafficking and domestic servitude, and commercial sexual exploitation (sex trafficking). Human trafficking occurs when an individual is employed for little to no pay for their employers' benefit. Labor trafficking and domestic servitude are most commonly associated with migrant workers, and in-home services such as nannies and housekeepers. Sex trafficking occurs under the guise of prostitution.

Trafficking

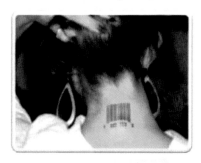

Now that we have looked at smuggling, prostitution and human trafficking as separate issues, we can now see how they often overlap one another. An individual who is smuggled into this country is here illegally and therefore has limited options for employment. So someone who is smuggled may turn to prostitution to support themselves, or they can become a trafficked person as they work for illegal wages and experience maltreatment by their employer. And likewise, prostitution often either indicates or causes additional vulnerabilities which could cause an individual to be trafficked.

Giving Life!! #thanksdaddy

After working all night in an unsafe environment, his victim is grateful for a fast food meal.

The human trafficking laws were originally authorized in 2000 as a part of the Trafficking Victims Protection Act (TVPA). According to 18 U.S. Code Chapter 77 Section 1591 – Sex Trafficking of Children or by force, fraud, or coercion, human trafficking is defined as:

> *The act of recruiting, harboring, transporting, providing, or obtaining for the purpose of labor, services or sexual acts through force, fraud or coercion for exploitation, slavery or any commercial sex act with a minor.*

Let's take a closer look at each piece of this law.

... THE ACT OF RECRUITING, HARBORING, TRANSPORTING, PROVIDING, OR OBTAINING

Knowingly acting in a way to entice or hire, house, drive, deliver or get an individual is committing the crime of human trafficking. The human trafficking laws were written fairly loosely, which allows law enforcement and the court system to effectively prosecute traffickers that have a wide variety of tactics and level of involvement. For example, "harboring" can be as extreme as locking someone inside a house or room, or as seemingly harmless as providing a place for them to stay.

Hello Amy, a, girl of your caliber should be doing big things in a major way. If your interested traveling, being in a better situation, being on a better team, making more money, having professional photos, classy website & a upscale incall locations to work from let me know.

A pimp attempts to recruit a prostituted woman.

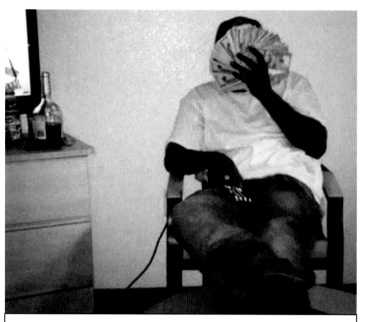

Waiting with his victim in her hotel room, a pimp casually shows the profits of his exploitative tactics.

A trafficker seeks to use an individual's labor for their own profit. When a trafficker actions indicate their intention of benefitting financially from their work, it is human trafficking. When a trafficker and their victim are pulled over in a traffic stop, or questioned during an undercover operation, a trafficker's first response is typically one of denial: they will claim that they had no idea what their victim was doing, or deny receiving any form of payment.

... THROUGH FORCE, FRAUD OR COERCION,

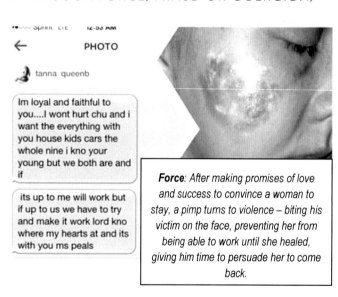

tanna_queenb

Im loyal and faithful to you....I wont hurt chu and i want the everything with you house kids cars the whole nine i kno your young but we both are and if

its up to me will work but if up to us we have to try and make it work lord kno where my hearts at and its with you ms peals

Force: *After making promises of love and success to convince a woman to stay, a pimp turns to violence – biting his victim on the face, preventing her from being able to work until she healed, giving him time to persuade her to come back.*

(pimp) in ur life already but if ur a free agent then I would love to get know u as a person and see wat kind of beautiful things we could put together as a team.im not a pimp im just a hustler who loves to get $ in multiple ways I dont wanna make $ off u I wanna make money with u 50/50 if ur good at managing ur own $ if not then I think its best I handle all financial issues,im from seattle but I

Fraud: *a trafficker attempts to recruit a prostituted woman, promising not to exploit her, but to be her partner.*

A trafficker's initial method of recruiting appears to be a successful business person, or caring romantic partner. Oftentimes, they make promises of wealth, possessions, love, or anything else to lure a vulnerable person in. Once their victim commits to working for them or being their intimate partner, the relationship slowly shifts to abuse and exploitation.

> "I was 12 and already in The Game, I was that girl with no family, no direction ..."
>
> - "Princey"

Before the 2000 TVPA, children were arrested and prosecuted along with adults engaging in prostitution. As our society has learned more about commercial sexual exploitation, is has become increasingly obvious to law enforcement and prosecutors that no child is willingly involved in prostitution. So the terms "child prostitute" and "juvenile prostitute" are being dropped from legal and court language, and replaced with phrases such as "exploited child" or "trafficked juvenile" to indicate their lack of ability to consent to such activities. As a result, any child that is found to be involved in a situation involving commercial sex is automatically removed from the situation and their abuser arrested and prosecuted with no additional evidence or testimony required. When it comes to minors, a trafficker cannot use the defense of not knowing that the person was a minor, nor can they claim that the child consented to the activities.

 KEY POINT: IT IS NEVER OK TO PURCHASE AND HAVE SEX WITH CHILDREN.

The TVPA was passed as a part of the Victims of Trafficking and Violence Protection Act of 2000. This legislation  included the official definition of human trafficking, and mandated annual reports for states and countries, policies for interagency task forces, minimum standards and expectations, and protection and assistance for victims of trafficking. It also included actions against governments that fail to meet the minimum standards, increased prosecution and punishment of traffickers, and assistance to foreign countries to meet the minimum standards.

In 2003, the TVPA was reauthorized and included policy to combat international sex tourism, termination of international contracts and grants with businesses that take part in exploiting persons, assistance for family members, and allows victims to pursue a civil suit against their trafficker. This reauthorization also added additional support and strengthened sanctions for the exploitation of minors, and allocated resources for research on the issue.

U.S. Laws on Trafficking in Persons

The Victims of Trafficking and Violence Protection Act of 2000 (P.L. 106-386), the Trafficking Victims Protection Reauthorization Act of 2003 (H.R. 2620), the Trafficking Victims Protection Reauthorization Act of 2005 (H.R. 972), and the Trafficking Victims Protection Reauthorization Act of 2008 (H.R. 7311) provide the tools to combat trafficking in persons both worldwide and domestically. The Acts authorized the establishment of G/TIP and the President's Interagency Task Force to Monitor and Combat Trafficking in Persons to assist in the coordination of anti-trafficking efforts.

The reauthorization in 2005 included enhanced protection under the "T" visa, additional activities to monitor and combat forced and child labor, prevention measures, the establishment of a grant program to focus on the issue of trafficking, and enhancing state and local efforts.

In 2008, the reauthorization included protection for victims from retaliation and to ensure their availability to testify against their trafficker, assistance for trafficking victims, additional penalties against traffickers, and accountability measures for the US government.

The most recent reauthorization was in 2013, and included the Violence Against Women Act. Specifically for trafficking victims, the act included strengthening partnerships between agencies and law enforcement on a nationwide, state, and local levels, the addition of best practices in working with trafficking victims, and protection for domestic workers and other nonimmigrants.

When the Trafficking Victims Protection Act was passed, the public jumped eagerly at this initiative as images of extreme abuse and stories of unthinkable manipulation were portrayed in the name of punishing predators that violate the innocence of children. The TVPA certainly offers more specific protection for exploited minors than the Mann Act did; it provides strengthened sentences for those convicted of trafficking a minor, and changed the age of consent for the commercial sex industry from 15 to 18. Now, any minor is determined to be a victim, which is most certainly a step in the right direction.

Unfortunately, the Department of Justice reported that in the first eight years, only about 2000 victims were rescued. And only a portion of those victims were children. While it is imperative to remember that even one child victim is too many, the cost associated with the rescuing of these victims has been called into question. During those 8 years, about $1.5 billion was allocated for the Trafficking Victims Protection Act. To put this into perspective, according to national statistics, children who are in the foster care system cost about $12,000 per child. If the main goal of the TVPA is to rescue victims, then it has cost about $750,000 to rescue each trafficking victim, and we must remember that most of these funds do not even go to any actual care and rehabilitation of the victims themselves. Considering the foster care system is where many sex trafficked minors come from in the first place, it would make much more sense to focus these funds on prevention strategies.

The State Department claims that at the most, only 1% of the estimated victims had been identified during the first ten years of the Trafficking Act. This means that either their original numbers were grossly over-estimated, or the methods we are using to find victims are not effective. "R.S" is a JD/MBA graduate with a successful legitimate business in addition to his experience as a pimping women for the last seven years. In a brief interview he explained, "For a law that was meant to protect minors, it [affects] a lot more entities other than minors, which is where the legislation is flawed. I think if they took the time to … identify who they are after … the law may be more effective." With the popularity of online prostitution, minors potentially end up going undetected, and a large number of consenting adults involved end up affected by the increased undercover operations.

With protecting the innocence of minors being at the forefront of the Trafficking Victims Protection Act, it is discouraging to face the fact that these laws are simply not bringing out the desired results. Part of the TVPA's goal is to clarify that all children involved in the sex trade are victims, and should not be treated as criminals. Operation Cross Country, the nationwide bust carried out each summer, in 2013, was carried out in 77 cities across the country, and the FBI rescued 105 children. However, a majority of the children rescued ended up being placed either in jail facilities or with foster families. Placing these children right back into the system that let them down in the first place does nothing but start this cycle over again.

In addition to the federal charge of human trafficking, traffickers can be charged with many other crimes.

Federal Charges:

- RICO
- Mann Act
- PROTECT Act
- National Defense Authorization Act

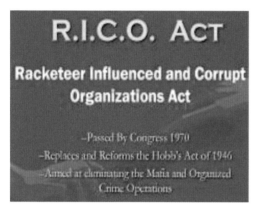

Other charges including state and local charges can include pimping and pandering, improper use of interstate commerce, managing or owning a prostitution business, conducting or directing someone to a place for the purpose of prostitution, permitting another person to use a place under their control for the use of prostitution, or keeping or leasing a house for the purpose of prostitution.

STATE RATINGS FOR HUMAN TRAFFICKING LAWS

| 2011 | 2012 | 2013 | 2014 |

From 2011 to 2014, Polaris Project rated each state here in the US on their human trafficking laws and efforts to combat commercial exploitation. As you can see, states are passing legislation and putting policy into action to help prevent and respond to human trafficking. Polaris rates each state on how well they are doing with sex and labor trafficking laws, asset forfeiture, investigative tools, training for law enforcement, task forces, no requirement of proof for exploited minors, civil remedies, the posting of a state resource hotline, safe harbor for minors, victim assistance, and vacating convictions for victims.

KEY POINT: IN THE LEGAL ARENA, WE ARE MOVING IN THE RIGHT DIRECTION, BUT WE STILL HAVE A LONG WAYS TO GO.

If you think back to the beginning of this book, where we looked at what the media and pop culture, part of the problem with the images portrayed as a sex trafficking scenario, and the characters illustrated is that it often allows us to think that we are exempt from being at risk. The most important piece of preventing sex trafficking from ever occurring is understanding that ANY person is at risk for exploitation.   We all have vulnerabilities in our life, or encounter situations throughout life that make us susceptible to being preyed upon. Take a few moments to answer the *Understanding Vulnerabilities Questionnaire* on this page before we start looking at vulnerable populations and risk factors. Chances are, you or someone you know has experienced a majority of the scenarios on the questionnaire. The vulnerabilities listed here are only a handful of the risk factors that can lead someone to be taken advantage of and exploited.

Understanding Vulnerabilities Questionnaire

Have you or someone you know:

Experienced feelings of loneliness or depression?	YES	NO
Been bullied?	YES	NO
Lost a family member?	YES	NO
Contemplated, attempted, or committed suicide?	YES	NO
Been robbed?	YES	NO
Been sexually assaulted?	YES	NO
Had a lot of debt?	YES	NO
Shared personal information on social media?	YES	NO
Been in this country illegally?	YES	NO
Had problems in an intimate relationship?	YES	NO
Been a runaway or experienced homelessness?	YES	NO
Been involved in child welfare services?	YES	NO
Received financial support from human services?	YES	NO
Experienced racism or discrimination?	YES	NO

The fact is, there is no one factor or scenario that guarantees an indvidual's likelihood of being trafficked. Denying or ignoring the potential for exploitation puts inviduals at risk. Being aware of the risk factors and indicators of trafficking can help protect yourself and your family.

It is natural to want to know how to protect ourselves from harm – what people and situations to circumvent. However, be careful when approaching the topic of "causes", especially with victims and survivors, and avoid asking questions such as "What did you do to get trafficked?" This is **victim-blaming**: asserting that the victim had control over what a perpetrator did to them,

or could have somehow prevented their victimization. Do NOT victim blame. Blaming the victim removes accountability from the trafficker, and puts the responsibility on the victim.

The rape awareness movement has made huge strides in helping society shift its perspective on sexual assault – that it is not the victim's fault that they dressed a certain way, consumed alcohol, or were in a particular location. Sex assault is a large portion of the trauma sex trafficking victims endure, and so we must treat trafficking victims with the same compassion as we do a rape victim, because they are essentially a victim of on-going, repeated rapes. Victim blaming in circumstances of commercial sexual exploitation is a serious piece of the problem in our society, because we spend more time telling women how to avoid being trafficked than we do teaching men not to exploit. Likewise, the circumstances that a victim experiences prior to being trafficked are beyond their control, and so to imply that they could have stopped being trafficked would also imply that they could have stopped, for example, child abuse or generational poverty.

If you see or hear victim blaming of a prostituted woman taking place, do not remain silent – speak out! Talk to your friends, start a discussion to challenge the thought patterns of friends and coworkers. If someone justifies the exploitation of women because she "has daddy issues," educate them not only on their victim-blaming mentality, but on the truth of commercial sexual exploitation.

No one deserves to be trafficked, or sexually assaulted repeatedly for years. Unless we start shifting the cultural perspective, we will continue to excuse the predators in our society. We are all a part of the solution to the culture of victim blaming.

People currently facing exploitation come from every citizenship status – US citizens, foreign nationals, immigrants and refugees. The most vulnerable people groups are those with complex emotional, psychological, and financial vulnerabilities, which is why youth in general but more specifically runaways, child abuse victims, and those in the child welfare system are considered very high risk. Other high risk populations include single parents, assault survivors, domestic

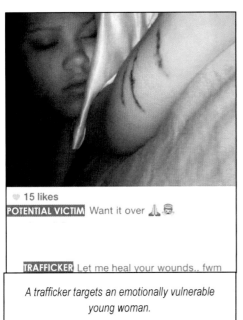

❤ 15 likes
POTENTIAL VICTIM Want it over ⚖🛢

TRAFFICKER Let me heal your wounds.. fwm

A trafficker targets an emotionally vulnerable young woman.

violence victims, individuals in regions of war or conflict, those who experience social discrimination or are facing economic uncertainty, and individuals struggling with substance abuse and addiction.

Referring back to the previous page about victim-blaming, it is important to understand how a trafficker operates. Pimps will prey on the most vulnerable in society, for the simple fact that they need the most help, and have access to the least amount of resources. For example, a youth who runs away from an abusive home and finds themselves homeless will typically go to a public place for safety and shelter such as a mall or bus stop. Traffickers know that a scared and hurt child with no one to turn to will be looking to have their basic needs of food and shelter met, in addition to being protected, loved, and given a future to hope for. So – NO, it is not the youth's fault they were abused, nor is it their fault that they trusted a kind stranger promising a home and a hot meal. Rather, it is a series of events that a trafficker waits for patiently, and preys when the child is the most vulnerable. A series of events that create layers of vulnerabilities can occur to anyone at any time in their life, and traffickers are not only expert manipulators and masters of disguises, but they are also opportunists – they are constantly on the prowl, waiting for a situation to present itself. In summary, anyone with a lack of education or opportunity can be preyed upon, as well as anyone with a desire to be loved, cared for or protected.

KEY POINT: YOU AND I CAN BE EXPLOITED FOR OUR VULNERABILITIES, TOO.

A majority of the sex trafficking cases we read about in articles or watch on the news feature stories of extreme physical abuse, however most sex trafficking cases involve what is commonly known as the "Romeo pimp" or "boyfriend pimp." This is important to understand because the process of finding and exploiting a victim is most often a long process, taking weeks, months and sometimes even years, rather than a kidnapping and torture until compliance. The reason for this is two-fold: the investment and return ratio, and the legal implications. First of all, a victim who is kidnapped and tortured into compliance requires around-the-clock supervision, transportation and repeated abuse. This type of victim will more than likely run at their first chance, because they are consciously aware of the fact that they do not want to be there. A victim who is lured in with false promises of love, fame, and success is much more likely to insist they are participating willingly, and to deny allegations that they are being taken advantage of. When it comes to legal implications, it is much easier in court for a victim to prove they were trafficked and exploited if they bear the physical evidence of torture and abuse. It is much more difficult for a jury to believe a victim who only has the mental and emotional scars. Traffickers know these things, which is why they commonly coerce their victims into believing they have a choice in the matter. In fact, once a trafficker has recruited a victim, they call the process "choosing" to reinforce the belief that it is the victim's choice to be under their control.

There have been cases where a trafficker will begin the recruiting and grooming process when an individual is a minor, and continue it for up to two years before beginning to exploit them. A trafficker might do this for one of two reasons: the level of investment indicates the potential profit, and for legal reasons. Again, traffickers know that the amount of time, attention and money they invest in their product up front, the larger the dividends as the victim may remain loyal to them for their supposed generosity many years. They also are aware of the current trafficking laws here in the US, and that they will do felony time in federal prison for exploiting a minor, with or without evidence. Oftentimes a situation involving commercial sexual exploitation goes unidentified because, unless the people around the victim know the signs to look for, the situation may appear to be a strained intimate relationship or a rebellious teen, or trafficking may not even be considered a possibility because the victim's support network has known the predator for so long that they would never assume something so horrific was occurring.

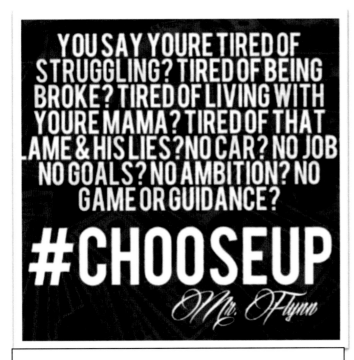

A trafficker advertises on social media.

A trafficker's act of **recruiting** involves using an enticing offer to cast a net with the hopes of generating interested individuals. That may be posting an ad in a newspaper or online offering employment as a model or an escort. It may also be directly contacting prostituted women with promises of better living and working conditions. Recruiting may also be much more focused and involve targeting a specific individual in a public place such as a mall, school or bus stop. Traffickers know where naïve or vulnerable people may hang out, and will target those places, hoping to find their next victim. It is also not uncommon for traffickers to drive through neighborhoods where they know there are group homes, waiting for a youth to run away, and then lure them in with promises of love, a warm meal, or a place to stay.

Once a trafficker has targeted an individual through their recruitment process, they begin the **grooming** phase. This phase can last as long as several years as a trafficker develops a strong relationship and position in their victim's life before they begin to exploit them. Think about it: the longer someone is a regular part of our life, the more likely it is that we trust them, and have shared more about ourselves with them. The first step in the grooming process is to identify a vulnerability. Traffickers are incredibly intelligent criminals with sociopathic tendencies. They are able to zero in on a person's wants and needs through a series of conversations with them, which helps them figure out how exactly to present themselves. The second step in grooming is to become significant – posing most commonly as a boyfriend or father-figure, or making the victim feel they are needed. The more important an individual is in our life, the more often we take their advice, confide in them, and feel safe with them. The third step is to create additional vulnerabilities or an obligation to the predator, which could include creating or supporting a substance abuse problem, getting their victim pregnant, or using shame, threats and blackmail. There are also instances of traffickers helping their victim get clean from drugs, or encouraging their victim to go to college on student loans, both of which situations are interpreted as the trafficker being helpful, and then the victim is manipulated into believing that they owe their trafficker their life, are indebted to them, or need to work to somehow pay them back. These additional vulnerabilities and obligations hold a victim in the life circumstances that they are in, and make them feel as though they cannot turn to their family, friends, or other support system for help, or that they do not need anyone else's help because their trafficker has proven themselves to be an excellent leader and caregiver. This leads to the fourth step, which is to remove the credibility of others. By isolating their victim, and using a series of events to illustrate that others in the victim's life do not care, or cannot help, the victim turns towards the trafficker as their sole source of information and care. The final step is to begin exploiting the victim through  commercial sex. A trafficker may follow these steps in the process in the order listed, or they may rotate through them repeatedly to create layers of trauma and vulnerabilities, ensuring their victim remains their captive.

Through this recruiting, grooming and exploiting process, a victim is subjected to constant violence, severe physical and emotional trauma, degradation and dehumanization, and complete financial dependence. Like Pavlov's dogs, who after being repeatedly presented with a piece of meat while hearing a bell ring, they eventually came to salivate at the sound of the bell, even when there was no meat, a victim learns that absolute obedience is the best way to survive, and that it will occasionally bring a "reward." The long-term abuse disrupts the individual's ability to think, feel, and act, and their brain shifts into a purely survival mode. A victim's entire day is often focused on getting their basic needs met – such as eating. Things like praise and attention can often become to be viewed as special treatment or a reward for good behavior.

Trauma and abuse that are experienced for an extended period of time can create a trauma bond between the trafficker and their victim, making it difficult for the victim to leave, as their trafficker has become their entire world, and their sole place for love, affection, and care. For a majority of trafficking victims, they do not identify as victims during their time of exploitation, and identify with their abuser's mission and methods. This is most commonly known as Stockholm's syndrome, and one of the most notorious cases of such is Patty Hearst. A billionaire heiress, she was kidnapped and tortured. She then accompanied her captors to a series of bank robberies, and took part in committing the crimes. When the group was finally apprehended, Patty spit in the police officer's face and called them "pigs." This came as a shock to everyone, as they expected to find Patty a grateful victim, glad to be rescued. As a billionaire heiress, Patty had no need to commit these robberies, and this illustrates the amount of mind control and the shift in her perspective as the isolation and trauma persisted.

"The Game" demands absolute obedience of its victims.

The pimp culture and belief system has countless rules and its own form of punishments and guidelines for behavior. Once a victim has been exposed to this culture for an extended period of time, there is a considerable amount of brainwashing that occurs. In fact, it is the Free Our Girls' organizational perspective that the pimp culture meets every characteristic of a cult, and it sometimes helps people understand a victim's mentality when they think of working with a cult member, and helping them deprogram and reintegrate into society. (Be on the lookout for a book that investigates these characteristics, social structure, and entrenched beliefs in 2016) We so badly want to help victims – kick down doors, and carry them to safety – however a "rescue" is less likely to be effective, rather walking alongside a victim while they *find their freedom* has more lasting results.

 KEY POINT: MENTALLY AND EMOTIONALLY MANIPULATING AN INDIVIDUAL IS MORE PROFITABLE AND OFFER THE TRAFFICKER A LITTLE MORE LEGAL

INDICATORS

Depending on who you are, and how you may come into contact with a victim, there are different physical and social indicators to be aware of. While these indicators, individually, do not necessarily mean a person is definitely being trafficked, they are red flags that can and should add up to give you reason to look further into the situation.

Physical indicators include: possessions, environment, and their body. Possessions are a great indicator – either a lack of them, or specific possessions. An individual that you believe is prostituted, and even perhaps claims to be taken care of by another person, yet lacks their identification, weather-appropriate clothing, or other general belongings can be an indicator. On the other end of the spectrum, many trafficking victims possess several phones (often prepaid models), prepaid gift cards, condoms and lubricant and hotel key cards. Other possessions that are easily

While not criminal individually, the combination of prepaid gift cards, prepaid phones, and condoms can be enough indicators to warrant further investigation of an individual's situation.

observable are a young person who has their hair and nails done, and wears nice clothing, purses and accessories yet has no legitimate form of employment. If you are able to learn more about their working and living conditions and find that either or both are poor, this could indicate exploitation. Again, these conditions could be purely visible in the form of filth, drug paraphernalia, or a lack of proper materials such as blankets, food and hygiene products. Or they could require a little deeper look, such as finding out that an individual is working and sleeping in the same hotel room, meaning that they sleep at night in the same bed they were exploited in all day. Discovering whether a victim feels safe their surroundings – the places they work and live, and the people they are around. If you are a health care professional and observe signs of abuse, injuries consistent with sexual assault or the individual tests positive for an STI, follow up the exam with some

questions about their work or home life, intimate partner(s), children, and observe any other physical or social indicators explained here. And lastly, tattoos are often visible on the bodies of victims. The most common tattoos are references to money such as the dollar sign, a name or initials, crowns, chess pieces, references to a king, royalty or loyalty, and even hashtags with acronyms. These tattoos are placed on a victim's neck, chest, shoulder blade, fingers, behind the ear, on the breast, buttocks or in the pelvic region, or forearm. Physically, a victim may have a lack of freedom to come and go, which could be physical chains or some other form of captivity, but it could also mean emotional, psychological or financial chains, which are invisible until you start talking with the individual to see if they are free to come and go as they want or need.

Social indicators include isolation and withdrawal, and are often most noticeable by their immediate social circle when they first start, such as a victim who was regularly attending school or taking part in activities with their friends, and then suddenly begins to isolate and withdraw from those around them. They may become truant or drop out of classes, stop attending church or social group meetings, and make excuses for why they could not attend. A victim's language will often change to include slang and acronyms that describe sexual services, and phrases used in the pimp culture. Appendix A contains a list of these commonly used slang, acronyms and phrases, and their definitions. Younger

"LITTLE GIRL LOST"

Mommy ... daddy ... someone help me.
Can you hear me? Do I matter? Is my pain real?
I look left ... I turn right ... But it's dark ... And no one's in sight.
So I run ... as fast as I can ... falling right into the arms of a man
Who's really a beast. He takes my heart, mind, body ... And soul ... as has his feast.
So I'm left with nothing just an empty shell ... Little girl lost ... in a 5 by 10 jail cell ... Welcome to hell.

"I was molested from the time I was 9 until the age of 12 by the son of my foster parents. At the age of 12, I left that hell I called home and turned to the streets. I met a guy who was much older who quickly became my boyfriend who had me selling cocaine. I continued to go to school because that was my only connected to still being a kid. The man who had raped me for all those years had destroyed everything inside of me. I've been in The Game since 16 – I have been raped, robbed, kidnapped, stabbed up, beat near to death, sold to other pimps as punishment. At 18 I was federally indicted with my pimp and even though I was a young girl – mentally, spiritually and physically destroyed - they charged me for helping him recruit other women."

- Brittney C, Survivor

girls may suddenly have an older boyfriend that spoils them with gifts and trips to nice restaurants and house parties. Minors may run away from home to be with a trafficker that has already targeted and recruited them and begun the grooming process. Individuals may present with STI's or an unplanned pregnancy, both of which indicate high risk sexual activity. And finally, Internet and social media interactions contain language and conversations that indicate they may have been targeted as a vulnerable individual. Appendix B contains more information on common websites and smart phone apps that are used by traffickers, and what to look for in communications.

 KEY POINT: IF YOU SEE SOMETHING, SAY SOMETHING!

AWARENESS: REVIEW AND REFLECT

1. *What is the difference between trafficking and smuggling?*

2. *What is the difference between sex work and trafficking?*

3. *How are victims recruited and controlled?*

4. *Where might you encounter a victim in your day-to-day life?*

5. *What are some of the reasons victims may be reluctant to try to escape or report a crime?*

6. *What crimes might law enforcement respond to that might warrant a closer look for potential victims of trafficking?*

7. *What health issues might medical professionals encounter that might warrant a closer look for potential victims of trafficking?*

8. *What social situations might educators encounter in their classrooms that might warrant a closer look for potential victims of trafficking?*

9. *Can you recall a past case or situation that included possible indicators that you may have missed last time? What will you do differently in the future should a similar situation present itself?*

PREVENTION

[pri-**ven**-sh*uh* n]

noun

1. the act of preventing; effectual hindrance

We can have all the response policies and procedures in the world, but if we do not have a prevention plan, our girls will continue to be exploited.

PREVENTION

Commercial sexual exploitation affects every social and professional sphere within a community. Sex trafficking <u>can</u> be prevented. This requires a combination of efforts. There are three main groups of individuals at the center of the issue of human trafficking: the buyers, the sellers, and the product. We must address each of these segments in the same avenues, but with different tactics. When it comes to preventing sex trafficking, we must first educate, then address voids, and challenge stereotypes. We must use this approach with all three segments of the issue of commercial sexual exploitation.

EDUCATION

When Free Our Girls was first founded, the initial plan was to start prevention programs with at-risk youth, and to begin working with victims and survivors in our area. When we started connecting with local agencies and community resources, we got one of two responses: "Human trafficking? Isn't that, like the immigrants in shipping containers?" or "Human trafficking? Oh yes, that's horrible, good thing it doesn't happen in small towns like ours!" In fact, in 2014, the official statement from law enforcement in our area on the issue was "statistics on trafficking do not exist, and therefore we do not have a problem" – can you see how backwards that is?! We quickly realized that we needed to take a giant step back and begin with educating our community. And so the Human Trafficking Awareness, Prevention & Response training was created, with the goal of teaching parents, high-contact industry employees, and the general public what human trafficking and commercial sexual exploitation were – how to recognize the signs and identify an at-risk or currently exploited individual. Our training meets the objectives as outlined by the Department of Homeland Security, listed at the beginning of this book. While there are many organizations that offer human trafficking education, we are the only organization that offers a certification card upon completion of the course. Your certificate of completion can be found in the back of this book, and is an excellent addition to your resume. Right now, this training is voluntary, but it is one of Free Our Girls' long-term goals to see this training and certification to become mandatory by law for high-contact industry employees – education is *that* important.

This training is available to the general public, but is primarily aimed at educating those who come into contact with victims of commercial sexual exploitation, the supply. Free Our Girls also speaks to various groups in the area such as the Journey Young Women's Conference, and speaks to high school aged girls about what a possible trafficker may say or do, where they are most likely to hang out, and how to protect themselves and their friends. In light of our strong caution against victim blaming, we focus on equipping young ladies with the tools and skills necessary to have healthy relationships, set boundaries, and to advocate for themselves, but we also partner with various organizations and faith-based groups to speak to boys and men about the damage caused by sex trafficking, and encouraging them to be protectors rather than exploiters.

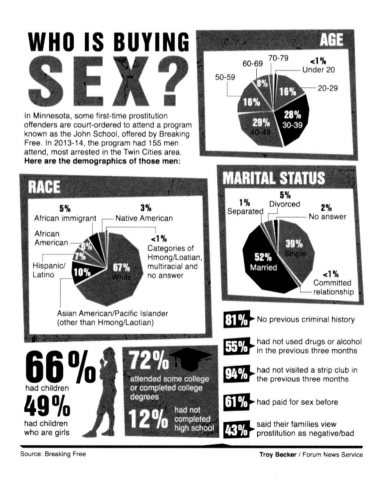

One of the programs Free Our Girls is a part of in our local community is the Larimer County "john's school," which is for men who have been arrested for soliciting a prostitute (law enforcement poses as a prostituted woman online or in massage parlors and carry out an undercover operation). These busts are aimed at decreasing the demand side of the issue, and the john's school focuses on educating men on the truth behind a large portion of the commercial sex industry. In an 8-hour class, men learn the truth about prostituted women, the health risks associated with high-risk sex, understand how the brain changes with a sexual addiction, and hear Free Our Girls' director's story of exploitation with the hopes of humanizing the issue. Because those who solicit prostitutes typically do not fit the typical criminal profile – they are generally white, employed, college-educated, and often married with children – they are more likely to change their behavior patterns when they are educated on the reality of the industry they are taking part in supporting. John schools are popping up all over the nation, and while most have only been in existence for a few years, there is almost a complete lack of recidivism amongst those who complete the course. While john schools could technically be considered a response to the issue rather than a prevention measure, the belief in educating potential buyers on the reality of sex trafficking goes a long way to preventing future exploitation. A majority of the men who come through these programs are first time offenders, and while some have been consistently purchasing services from prostituted women for years, many have only started to pursue the idea. John schools often stop these men from going down a very dark path of secrecy, risky behavior, and continuing the abuse of the women they solicit. Because many have families that are affected by their arrest, the john school provides these men with information to take home to share with their wives and children that brings further awareness to the truth.

When it comes to educating traffickers, this is a piece that is hardly ever addressed, yet it plays an equal role in ending commercial sexual exploitation. All traffickers were once innocent children, just like their victims. More data is needed to get a better idea of the general demographics of a trafficker. Once we have this information, we can begin educating our children, and encouraging young boys to treat women with respect and dignity, to ask for help when they need it, and appropriate ways to deal with stress and anger. The key to educating traffickers is tied closely with challenging stereotypes, and the cultural shift that is happening in regards to the glorification of the pimp culture.

The first step to preventing human trafficking is knowing that it does exist – in big cities and rural communities, in urban or impoverished neighborhoods and affluent ones. And that victims come from all walks of life, experience different vulnerabilities, and are preyed upon by individuals with sociopathic and narcissistic tendencies. It is our responsibility, once we are educated on commercial sexual exploitation, to then educate those around us.

How You Can Educate Others About Human Trafficking:

- **Host an awareness training.** You can host a Free Our Girls' Human Trafficking Awareness, Prevention & Response training, or purchase group training materials.
- **Teach your children and students about cyber security.** Use Appendix B to talk with your children about how to and with whom they interact on the Internet, and use this information to screen their daily use.
- **Incorporate human trafficking education into your professional workspace.** Trainings, manuals, best practices, and other distributed information are great ways to teach employees and coworkers.
- **Continue learning about the issue and hearing stories of survival.** An excellent list of additional resources can be found in Appendix C.
- **Stay up-to-date.** Laws, best practices, and tactics change frequently. Set up Google alerts with appropriate key words.
- **Get plugged in with Free Our Girls.** You can "like" the Free Our Girls' Facebook page to receive regular notifications, and you can sign up for our newsletter for detailed information, stories, and important dates. We are always in need of volunteers to train, man event booths, and represent our organization.
- **Speak out.** Correct people's speech and beliefs by informing them of the truth behind commercial sexual exploitation.

 KEY POINT: EDUCATION EMPOWERS EXPLOITED & DISADVANTAGED PEOPLE.

ADDRESSING VOIDS AND SOLVING VULNERABILITIES

Many of the complex social and emotional issues that make a victim easy to exploit start many years prior to their trafficker ever knowing them, and must be resolved through community support and legislation. Again, by addressing the vulnerabilities of the supply, demand, and suppliers, we can see an overall reduction in domestic sex trafficking,

Free Our Girls is making headway in the rural areas of Colorado. As we have begun educating law enforcement officers, first responders, medical professionals, district attorney's office staff, probation officers and victim's advocates, we have seen a shift in the perspective of the issue of human trafficking, and the recognition of potential victims. And while recognizing victims currently being exploited is an important undertaking, so is recognizing those who are at risk in the future.

In 2015, Free Our Girls started working with several probation departments to offer our F.L.I.G.H.T Program (Finding Lasting Improvement and Growth through Holistic Transformation), a program that contains a series of workshops designed to educate and equip those most at risk. What we discovered was that while there are many screening tools for probation officers to use to identify the likelihood of an individual on probation being at risk for homelessness, domestic abuse, or drug relapse, there are currently no screening tools available to indicate an individual at risk for being trafficked. And so with the help of our licensed clinical social worker, we created the Commercial Sexual Exploitation Screening Indicator. This screening tool is available to probation departments, so if you know of a probation office that could use the CSESI to help identify those in need of intervention services in your area, please contact Free Our Girls using the contact information in the back of this book.

As mentioned in the previous section, the typical customer is a white, middle-class, college-educated, gainfully employed, married man. Understanding what drives demand is critical to decreasing this side of the equation, because as long as there is a demand, traffickers will continue to work to find the supply. Through stories from the many women we walk alongside, and the stories these men have shared in "john school", an overwhelming majority of them struggle with maintaining an authentic intimate relationship, for a wide variety of reasons. Some struggle with substance abuse or sexual addiction that has isolated them from their spouses, some feel socially awkward and shy. A majority have a deep-seated longing to be acknowledged – *to be seen*. The complexities of the male psyche are too much to discuss in-depth in this book, but working with men's groups through churches, community centers, and other social groups can help address the need to identify their own vulnerabilities and scenarios that trigger the need to attain dominance, seek comfort, or escape reality can help stop thought patterns in their tracks. In addition to that, counseling and mentoring for men and couples to strengthen their relationships are needed so that all parties have their needs met in that relationship.

While traffickers' demographics are in many ways much harder to generalize, they are, in summary, usually lacking other employment opportunities. A majority of traffickers grew up surrounded by prostitution and violence, and simply acknowledge it as a way to make a living. And again, as mentioned previously, many young traffickers are emulating what they see and hear in movies and in music, and believe that the pimp culture is an acceptable means to an end. When we raise our children to value human life, to respect one another, and to evaluate what our culture tells us, we equip our next generation with the ability to elevate themselves above sexually exploiting our most vulnerable.

Once we understand that we all have vulnerabilities, and that it can take a series of events to push or pull someone into an exploitative situation, we can take the steps necessary to address the voids, or eliminate them altogether.

How You Can Address Voids and Solve Vulnerabilities

- **Train or become a compassionate foster parent.** Understand that children removed from or given up by their parents come with a deep longing for love, family, and acceptance. Taking children in is NOT just a paycheck.
- **Comply with, or lobby for child support enforcement measures.** NEVER use child support as a means to control the other parent, as it places them in a financially vulnerable position. We currently have billions of dollars in child support arrears nationwide – a majority of single mothers are one decision, one unexpected expense away from prostitution. And let's raise up a generation of children who understand the full responsibility of unprotected sex and having children.
- **Provide alternatives and consequences in male-dominated industries.** With boom communities springing up all over the country, the oil-and-gas industry brings with it a wildly disproportionate gender ratio and disposable income to unprepared towns with inadequate infrastructure. Companies can educate their employees and impose a zero tolerance policy. Oil-and-gas companies can partner with the cities in which their employees work and live to provide positive outlets for time, energy and money.
- **End the glorification of exploitation.** The entertainment industry will respond in kind when we tell them what we no longer find acceptable.

 KEY POINT: MANY COMMUNITIES ARE STARTING THE BATTLE AGAINST SEX TRAFFICKING WITH NO FOUNDATION.

CHALLENGE STEREOTYPES

We cannot deny that in our tech-driven world, our society has a close and almost dependent relationship upon media. The Internet is a double-edged sword, a world of unknowns and anonymity, where predators lurk in every chat room, website, and app. But we are also able to use the same technology to check in with our children, monitor our school's security, and where law enforcement is able to execute investigations and gather evidence against predators such as traffickers. With the rapidly expanding access to the world through the Internet and social media, our society's fascination and glorification of the pimp culture is apparent everywhere we go.

As we mentioned in the beginning of this book, most people's perception of a prostituted woman is one of two extremes: it is either a glamourous lifestyle of luxury and love like in *Pretty Woman*, or disease-ridden and drug-addled like the reality show *Intervention*. Exploited women are often made fun of for having "daddy issues", or looked down upon for taking part in high-risk sexual activity. Conversely, young females often refer to each other as "bitches", "sluts" or "whores" in both playful and derogatory ways. All of these behaviors and the use of language normalize exploitative and abusive behavior, making it acceptable for women to be treated and referred to in this way. One excellent example of how normalized these types of behavior are is in the popular video game, Grand Theft Auto. One scene in this game allows the player to purchase a prostitute, have sex with her, kill her, and take the money back. While video games do not cause the use of prostitutes, rape, murder or robbery, they certainly go a long ways in desensitizing our youth to the seriousness of these acts.

Pop culture and the media sends our youth an incredibly mixed message when it comes to soliciting and purchasing prostituted women. Our society demands that if a man is masculine/successful/powerful enough, he would never have or want to pay for sex, yet countless song lyrics include the phrase "it ain't trickin' if you got it" (implying that if one has enough money, purchasing women for sexual gratification is entirely acceptable). The blockbuster movie *50 Shades of Gray* drives home the illusion that with enough money and fame, men can essentially purchase a live-in sex slave. And lastly, within the online communities devoted to evaluating and purchasing prostituted women, men refer to themselves as "hobbyists" and insist that they are not a part of the problem of sex trafficking because the women they solicit are "legally consenting adults." The truth of the matter for this last fact is that pimps instruct their women not to give mention to the fact that they are under the control of a trafficker when they are being used by a paying customer as the customer is then less likely to solicit them.

The most widely accepted and incorrectly glamorized piece of the supply-demand-supplier relationship is that of the pimp or trafficker. Pimp culture is widely accepted in our society, and the term "pimp" often conjures up images of a successful and powerful male, a well-connected thug or businessman. A simple search on Amazon reveals pimp costumes for both adults and children, listed under the categories of "Humorous Costumes" and "Sexy Costumes." Now that you've learned the truth behind commercial sexual exploitation and the cruel motives and methods of a trafficker, chances are you find pimp costumes neither humorous nor sexy. In addition to costumes on Amazon, there are also a plethora of books available for purchase from self-proclaimed pimps on how to successfully manipulate and exploit women, and how to apply the rules of pimp culture to one's life. There are television shows like "Pimp My Ride" which use the term to implicate a showy, upgraded version of what previously existed, and movies like Hustle and Flow, which glamorize the pimp culture and strongly suggest the ability to gain a successful legitimate career using the proceeds of exploiting women. And finally, nightclubs all over the nation mimic the annual "Pimp and Hoe Ball", an event where real traffickers bring their victims out to parade their products around in public, and award the most powerful or successful each year as "Pimp of the Year."

The best way to challenge cultural stereotypes is to vote your wallet. As a consumer, you have an incredible amount of say in what manufacturers and retailers design and sell.

How You Can Challenge Stereotypes

- **Tell Hollywood that you don't support their version of what a pimp is.** Don't watch movies that glorify traffickers or the objectification and exploitation of prostituted women.
- **Choose wisely the costumes and characters you emulate.** Avoid costumes that perpetuate the stereotypes of women in the adult entertainment industry, and their abusers.
- **Encourage your friends, classmates and coworkers to change their language and their product purchases.**

KEY POINT: YOU CAN FIGHT SEX TRAFFICKING EVERY DAY.

RESPONSE

[ri-**spons**]

noun

1. an answer or reply, as in words or in some action.

The response to suspected human trafficking by an oil-and-gas company is much different from that of a school teacher, which is why Free Our Girls tailors our trainings to meet the needs and issues of specific industry and community groups.

RESPONSE

Upon the completion of this book, you will now be equipped with the knowledge to respond to human trafficking and commercial sexual exploitation in your community. Once you recognize the signs of a victim or an abusive situation, you can take the next steps which are to reach out to the victim, respond to the perpetrator, and to report the incident.

RESPONDING TO THE VICTIM

Trafficking victims have learned through repeated abuse and manipulation from numerous people over the course of their life to trust no one, especially strangers. So if you are in a professional setting or position of authority where you suspect a patient, employee or student is being exploited, directly asking them if they are being trafficked will generally get you a response of denial. Instead, if you feel the individual may be responsive, ask questions about their living situation, guardian or intimate partner, or their travel and work. If you have had an on-going relationship with the individual, you more than likely are viewed as a person that could potentially be trusted to know the truth, even if it is not immediately.

When you are certain that you have contact with a trafficking victim, and they are ready to share with you, it is important to respond to them in an accepting, non-judgmental way – projecting your thoughts and feelings and what you feel the individual should do to get out of the situation are often viewed as intrusive, and if you personally have not been in a similar situation, the victim will most likely believe that you have no idea what they are up against. It is for this reason, combined with the fact that a prostituted woman must make the decision on her own to want to leave, that you must allow the victim to lead the journey to freedom. Ask questions about how you can help them, what type of support they need, and any safety concerns they may have.

If and when a victim trusts you enough to open up and share a piece of their story with you, you will more than likely be horrified with the thought of how evil traffickers can be. This is a natural and normal reaction, however, displaying excessive shock, rage, or disbelief can overwhelm a victim in their most vulnerable moment. In addition, never challenge a victim's story, because as it is said – the truth is often stranger than fiction. Even if you feel some element of their story is exaggerated, telling a victim that you do not believe them only reinforces what their trafficker has continued to tell them – which no one will help.

Make sure that the victim knows that you are there to help them in any way that you can, and that you are a safe person and can provide them with a safe environment. Maintain the relationship with the victim long past the point in which they officially find their freedom. While they may have left the exploitive situation, the hard work has yet to begin. The journey to safety, healing and success is long and hard, and survivors need you as a vital piece of their support system as they learn whom to trust, how to ask for help, and that they are worthy of respect.

Once a woman has found freedom and has begun to rebuild her life, it is important to empower her and her family in any way that you can. If she is interested in becoming a survivor-leader, you can encourage her to write and speak at local events about her experiences (however do not push a survivor to publicly share her deepest wounds if she has no desire to do so). Make sure that she is compensated for her time and words – while a survivor's story is priceless, she does not deserve to be further exploited for her experiences. If an individual starts her own business or goes back to school, empower her by purchasing her products and services and telling your friends, and celebrate the completion of her certification or degree. Running a business or going to college are notable accomplishments for anyone, but for someone who has been told they would never amount to anything more than a product to be used for another's personal gain, these endeavors give a survivor an immense amount of confidence and personal satisfaction. In addition to the emotional and psychological gains of empowering a survivor by supporting their work and education efforts, you are also helping solve their financial vulnerabilities can safeguard them from exploitation in the future.

We often forget that a victim's positive network of friends and family need support and empowerment, too. While some parents know that their child is being trafficked, others may only have a small piece of the story, or even have no idea that this exploitation is occurring. In all of these instances, parents and family need support, encouragement and guidance for how to help their child, sibling, or friend find their freedom and begin healing. One resource Free Our Girls offers free of charge is an online support forum for families of victims and survivors, NEST (National Education and Support Team). This confidential community was identified as a nation-wide service gap, and we proudly host and monitor a safe place for individuals to find support on how to help the woman in their life who is dealing with exploitation. It is available upon referral from any human trafficking organization in the country. If you work with a local agency that has individuals to refer, or know of a family that could use the support, please contact Free Our Girls with the information listed in the back of this book.

RESPONDING TO THE PERPETRATOR

It can be tempting to intervene on behalf of a victim. We must strongly caution you to not approach the trafficker. This is important to understand for several reasons. Firstly, because of your own personal safety – traffickers are often armed and could become violent, quickly making a situation unpredictable. You also need to be aware of the victim's ultimate safety – trying to approach the trafficker in the hopes of freeing the victim will often backfire, and the consequences will rain down upon the victim. Victims are punished for confiding in anyone other than their trafficker, so it is best for both you and the victim if you resist the urge to show up at their house or hotel room, or create a public scene.

REPORTING THE SITUATION

In addition to the above reasons for not interacting with the alleged trafficker, should an altercation occur, or law enforcement be called to the immediate scene, there is often little evidence available for the police to corroborate your allegations against the trafficker. Instead, call the National Human Trafficking Hotline (1-888-373-7888), your local non-emergency law enforcement, or you can contact Free Our Girls to speak with someone for more information on how to handle the situation. When you make a report in this way, local law enforcement becomes aware of the potential situation and will do some investigation of the circumstances before approaching or arresting the trafficker. This ensures that the police are able to gather enough evidence and follow proper procedures to guarantee a solid case and subsequent conviction.

Despite our hopes, and what the news often tells us, many trafficking situations require time-consuming efforts behind the scenes before a plan is put into motion and a trafficker is arrested or a victim is able to find freedom (whether or not law enforcement becomes involved). It is easy to become discouraged, lose hope, find ourselves angry and frustrated, and want to give up. But don't – keep fighting! Maintain the relationship with the victim in whatever way you can, keep in contact with law enforcement or other agencies involved, and seek help for yourself as a person of support in the victim's life. Protect yourself and set personal boundaries to keep yourself from becoming overly emotionally involved (if possible), and be there to celebrate every step forward, no matter how long it takes.

KEY POINT: YOU MAY BE THE VICTIM'S ONLY LIFELINE.

PREVENTION & RESPONSE: REVIEW AND REFLECT

1. How does law enforcement handle these investigations?

2. What happens to the victims in your area once they are rescued? What resources are available?

3. Why might law enforcement and the community as a whole not be aware of this crime? How will you help change that?

4. What immediate needs should you anticipate that a victim may have?

5. What information in this book changed or challenged your assumption about sex trafficking?

6. How will you help?

APPENDIX A

Commonly used terms, acronyms and phrases.

The pimp culture is commonly referred to as *The Game* or *The Life*. Within this subculture is an entire language that you should be familiar with in order to help you recognize a potential victim.

TERMS

blew up – see *fired*

bread – another word for money, quota or trap.

break – prostituted women are taught to "break tricks", meaning to take or make money from customers. The victim is then expected to "break herself" to her pimp, meaning she must hand over all of the profits from the sexually exploitation

Choosey Susie – a prostituted woman who is re-trafficked repeatedly. The term implies this is her decision and responsibility.

choosing (or **choose up**) – indicates the alleged choice of the victim to be under the control of a trafficker

fag (or **faggot**) – a victim who tries to leave her trafficker, is re-trafficked repeatedly, attempts to prostitute independently, or violates a trafficker's household rules

fired – when a woman is able to get away from a trafficker, the trafficker will often state that she was fired to indicate his complete control over her ability to have freedom of movement

folks (or **P**) – a pimp or trafficker

free-fucking – having sex without receiving compensation, an activity that is only acceptable to those not in The Game

freelancing – refers to when a woman is sent to work in bars, restaurants, or casino floors

hoe – (or **ho**) – prostituted women refer to themselves and other prostituted women in this way

instruction – a woman under the control of a trafficker is said to be "under instruction"

knock – when a trafficker recruits a new victim and begins the grooming process

quota – the amount a trafficker requires his woman to make per day before she is allowed to come home. Also called a trap.

rack (or **stack**) – one thousand dollars

real one – refers to an individual who follows the rules of The Game, whose reputation for loyalty precedes them

renegade – a woman who prostitutes herself willingly and independently. These women are ostracized from those under the control of traffickers, as traffickers often fear that the women they control will decide they want to work independently as well.

simp – a weak pimp

snitch (or **rat**) – an individual who goes to law enforcement to report their trafficker, a violent customer, or other woman, etc.

square – any person or situation that is outside The Game

track (or **blade** or **boulevard**) – refers to street prostitution

trap – referring to the "trap spot" or "trap house" (previously a drug reference), the place a prostituted woman is exploited. Can also refer to the required nightly quota

trick – a paying customer

turn out – used to indicate a woman has just been recruited for the first time and is the process of being groomed. Also used to refer to a woman's first trafficker who introduced her to The Game

wife (or **wifey** or **wife-in-law**) – other women under the control of the same trafficker

ACRONYMS

16 – the sixteenth letter of the alphabet is "P", which refers to a pimp

304 – like the word games played on a calculator, when turned upside down, 304 spells "HOE", referring to a prostituted woman

AOB – All On a Bitch – refers to a trafficker placing the risk, blame, etc., on the victim

BB – bare back, indicating unprotected sexual act (BBBJ, for instance, would refer to oral sex on a customer without a condom) **

BFE – Boyfriend Experience – refers to boyfriend or Romeo pimps, who use the guise of an intimate relationship to gain control over a victim

BJ – blow job – oral sex**

FOE – Family Over Everything – placing family relationships over every other options in life

GFE – Girlfriend Experience – a sexual service requested by customers, indicating a level of intimacy typically not found in traditional street prostitution, and can include kissing, conversation, and unprotected oral sex**

HGO – (or **RHGO** or **CCHGO**) – Hoein' Goin' On (or Real Hoein' Goin' On., or Cross Country Hoein' Goin' On) – indicates a woman under the control of a self-proclaimed authentic pimp

MOB – Money Over Bitches – placing financial success over intimate relationships

MOE – Money Over Everything – placing financial success over every other option in life

PGO – (or **RPGO** or **CCPGO**) – Pimpin' Goin' On (or Real Pimpin' Goin' On., or Cross Country Pimpin' Goin' On) – indicates a self-proclaimed authentic pimp

*** There are numerous acronyms to describe specific sexual acts that customers solicit from prostituted women, not all of which are covered here.*

PHRASES

a prostitute with no instruction is headed for self-destruction – traffickers insist that in order to be involved in sex work, a woman must be the property of a pimp

as long as the outcome is income – high risk behavior is believed to be acceptable as long as it is financially beneficial

cash before ass – a motto used by traffickers to indicate that they will exploit their victim and coerce her into bringing the proceeds from prostitution back to him before he rewards her with love and affection

celebrate the money, not the bitch – to keep a victim constantly striving for affection and recognition, attention is diverted to their performance rather than the individual as a person

chances make champions – traffickers encourage their victims to take huge risks with their life and liberty with the illusion that it will all pay off

closed legs don't get fed – traffickers tell hesitant victims that they will be punished or have basic needs withheld if they do not obey

finesse over force – a statement made by traffickers to indicate they prefer to use fraud and coercion over force

fuck love get money – those indoctrinated into The Game begin to see how boyfriend/Romeo pimps use a woman's longing for love as a way to exploit her, and likewise traffickers will protect themselves from getting emotionally involved with the women under their control

get under the wing of a king – a trafficker's recruiting statement

go hard on a bitch – a trafficker's belief that he must abuse and exploit a victim as much as possible before rewarding her

hips, lips and fingertips – refers to the ways a victim can use their body and mind to make money from a customer

hoe up or blow up – a trafficker's recruiting statement

if it ain't foreign it's borin' – to indicate that foreign women are "exotic" and therefore more profitable. Also indicates the purchase of high-end fashion and cars.

in me, not on me – implies that the victim was born with an innate need to be exploited, or that the trafficker was born with the genetic makeup to be an exploiter

in/out of pocket – refers to a victim's behavior and interactions with others besides their trafficker. In pocket indicates good behavior, out-of-pocket indicates behavior that is justified through punishment

keep squares out your circle – a belief that those who do not understand or comply with the rules to The Game should not have relationships in any way with those who are in it

loyalty brings royalty – a common phrase traffickers use to coerce their victims into believing they will be following through on their promises for fame, success, love, etc.

money talks – a trafficker's belief that finances can be the solution to all problems

not all money is good money – for the prostituted woman, the justification to not pursue every customer. For the trafficker, the justification to get rid of one of his victims by selling or firing her for too many infractions (usually for using drugs, trying to leaves, is insecure in her needs for undivided attention from her abuser, etc.)

pimpin' ain't easy – a slogan made popular by the movie Hustle & Flow

proper instructions for proper productions – a trafficker's insistence that a prostituted woman must be under the control of a pimp in order to be profitable

real recognize real – those indoctrinated into The Game recognize phrases and beliefs amongst one another

show me the HoeFax – a term among the network of traffickers, indicating their interest in knowing how well a prostituted woman obeys and performs to determine if she is a product he would like to reap the profits from

slow feet don't eat – used to push victims to work hard to have their basic needs met

spend money to make money – the belief that investing in clothing, beauty products, cosmetic surgeries, high-end advertising websites, photo shoots, etc., will bring about higher paying customers

stay down for your crown – a trafficker's promise to their victim that following the rules will be rewarded

stay down to come up – a coercive statement from a trafficker indicating good behavior will be rewarded

stay in your lane – to mind one's own business, not interfere in another situation, or not to speak up when something is not right

stay ready so you don't have to get ready – the belief that a victim should always be ready to be sold to the highest bidder

take a chance to advance – a trafficker's attempt at recruiting

teamwork makes the dream work – justification for a trafficker to have multiple women under his control

ten toes down – can mean that a woman is under the control of a trafficker. Can also mean that a prostituted woman works on the track or freelances, as opposed to working in hotel rooms answering calls from online advertisements. Traffickers also refer to the number of women under their control by numbering their toes ("forty toes down" indicates a trafficker has four women under his control)

trust no one – The Game is a cut-throat culture, where everyone is just trying to survive

wake up to get your cake up – refers to the fact that a victim's entire day is often spent focused on making their quota

work smarter not harder – refers to forcing a victim to learn to steal, manipulate, and market themselves as high quality to make the most money in the least amount of time

APPENDIX B

Commonly websites and smart phone apps.

Backpage – www.backpage.com – the most notorious website in current times with numerous mentions in media and lawsuits. There is an Adult section with a variety of sub-sections including Escorts, Strippers, TS, and Body Rubs. Prostituted individuals will post ads selling their services (disguised as time & companionship). The section Adult Jobs often contains ads seeking "sugar babies" from prospective "sugar daddies", as well as traffickers posing as businessmen looking to hire new talent for their "modeling agency" or "escort service".

CityVibe – www.cityvibe.com – an "escort" directory set up and utilized in the same way as Craigslist and Backpage.

Craigslist - www.craigslist.com – while the "escorts" and "adult entertainment" are no longer sections, prostitution still occurs through the "personals" section. Women may post ads in the Women for Men section, or "johns" may post in the Men for Women section, or even the "Casual Encounters". The most common topics would be searching for a "sugar baby" or "sugar daddy", an individual in search of a one-time event to fulfill a specific fantasy or sex act. Women may post ads that appear to be a dating ad, but then lure men in with the hope of a long-term relationship. Men may also post ads that appear to be a dating ad, but then lure a vulnerable young woman in and then exploit her.

DateCheck – www.date-check.com – similar to P411, this site is more commonly used on the east coast, however it is used here in Colorado as well.

Dating Sites – www.chemistry.com, www.plentyoffish.com, www.match.com, www.eharmony.com, www.okcupid.com, www.zoosk.com, www.twoo.com, etc. These can be used similarly to individuals using the personals section of Craigslist.

Eros – www.eros.com – more popular in large cities, or to attract businessmen traveling from large cities in other states. This website features advertisements from "escorts" virtually all over the world.

P411 – www.p411.com – a nationwide screening site that verifies the legitimacy of both "johns" and "escorts". This site allows "johns" to send appointment requests to "escorts", and helps "escorts" stay safe.

Smartphone Apps – Tinder, Swipr, MeetMe, InstaBang, Sext App, Hinge etc. (search "dating" or "escorts" in the app store) – All of these are used with the guise of a dating relationship service, however are used by "escorts", "johns" and traffickers alike.

Social Media – Facebook (and Messenger), Twitter, Instagram, SnapChat, WhatsApp, Kik, Skype, Pinterest, Tumblr, etc. – All of these are used for purchasing and soliciting sexual services, as well as for recruiting victims.

Sugar Daddy Sites – www.seekingarangment.com, www.sugardaddyforme.com, etc. – These sites are used by "sugar daddy" and "sugar baby" individuals who are often just "johns" and "escorts" that are interested in a longer-term arrangement. Pimps also create profiles as "sugar daddies" to lure unsuspecting young women in.

The Erotic Review – www.theeroticreview.com – a nationwide advertising board and discussion forum similar to The Other Board. Often referred to as "TER". Men who frequent these types of boards call themselves "hobbyists" and take great pride in the number of reviews on different women they post.

The Other Board – www.theotherboard.com – now connected with Escort Boards (formerly www.escortphotos.net and www.escortboards.net), which are both primarily used here in Colorado, but also feature other states including Nevada. The Other Board (TOB) contains a section for "escorts" to post ads for their services, as well as a forum. The forum contains a discussion board which allows "escorts" and "johns" to discuss various topics related to sex, prostitution, etc. There are also private back-channel forums for both the men and women which allow them to share information regarding robberies and theft, underage activities, sex tourism, law enforcement operations, etc. The other part of the forum is a review board, which allows "johns" to rate the "escorts" they have seen, often detailing explicit activities.

APPENDIX C

Additional resources.

APPENDIX C

FOR THE GENERAL PUBLIC

ORGANIZATIONS

Polaris Project – www.polarisproject.org

National Human Trafficking Resource Center Hotline 1-888-373-7888

Truckers Against Trafficking – www.truckersagainsttrafficking.org

Colorado Organization for Victim Assistance (COVA) 303-861-1160

iEmpathize – www.iempathize.org

ADDITIONAL EDUCATIONAL MATERIALS

Tricked (2003) – documentary about prostitution and human trafficking available on Netflix

Hot Girls Wanted (2015) – documentary about the amateur porn industry

Boom (2015) – documentary about the oil boom communities in North Dakota, available through iEmpathize

The Making of a Girl (2006) – a survivor's story of being recruited and groomed, available on YouTube

FOR VICTIMS

Polaris BeFree Textline – Text "BeFree" (233733)

FOR SURVIVORS

GEMS (Girls Educational and Mentoring Services) – www.gems-girls.org

    Book – *The Survivor's Guide to Leaving* by Sheila White with Rachel Lloyd

    Online support forum

    Survivor-leadership conferences and opportunities

CASE STUDIES

A closer look at real-life scenarios of human trafficking.

MALINA

Malina* moved to the United States with her family as a child from Eastern Europe. After completing high school, her best friend and she were approached separately by pimps, who recruited them and begin the grooming process. In order to remain in the country, Malina's trafficker married her. She remained under his control for 6 years. During that time, she had several forced abortions, was beaten, raped, and robbed. One day, while working in a hotel room with one of the other women under his control, she made her quota for the day and left it with her wifey. She ran away, to another city in another state, with the help of one of her customers, and continued working in prostitution to get her own place to live. There, she was approached by a local music artist, who promised her protection, wealth and fame. Malina was re-trafficked for another 5 years by this man, who was a devout Muslim and encouraged her to convert as well. Her first pimp refused to sign the papers for a legal divorce, and the court battle took over two years to complete. Over the course of these 11 years, Malina has three felony convictions in three different states, and misdemeanors in at least five states. She owns nothing, and is repeatedly faced with threats of being deported when she is arrested.

LERA

Lera was the daughter of a wealthy European businessman, and after completing her bachelor's degree of science in Europe, her father arranged a marriage for her so that she could come to the US. Once per year, she met with her legal husband to take photos and spend the day together to help legitimize their relationship to immigration authorities. He was a nice man, but the marriage was a business transaction. Lera was enrolled in school and spent the remainder of her time partying with friends and traveling at her father's expense.

Lera's friend, Sarah, new a man who when by "R". Sarah told Lera that R was just a friend and successful businessman, and Lera had no reason to not trust Sarah. Unbeknownst to Lera, Sarah had been briefly under the control of R as he had trafficked her across the southern US. So when R approached Lera through a Facebook private message, Lera was friendly and interested in what this handsome, charming man had to say.

R told Lera that she should fly across the country to where he lived, that he had a job for her. He promised her all she had to do was go out to dinners, shows, and nightclubs with rich men and they would pay her. Lera soon booked a flight. When she arrived, R sent her with his other women to learn how to work the bars, casinos and hotels in the area. Her accent and exotic look made her highly desirable by traveling businessmen. What R didn't tell Lera was that she would have to have sex with these men in order to make the money he had promised, and he also neglected to tell her that he would be in complete control of her finances and movements. For two years, Lera was trafficked all over the US. Hotel and casino concierge begin calling Lera when high-end customers came into town, helping to arrange the sexual transactions. Lera was arrested several times, and each time, she was threatened with being deported. Her family did not know what she was caught up in, and she was terrified that someone would find out her secret life that she was trapped in.

JENNIFER

From Canada, Jennifer was brought into the US on a legitimate work visa by her trafficker. When her visa expired, she was not allowed to return to Canada or apply for another, which severely limited her options for employment outside of the sex industry. After having her first child with her trafficker, she left him, realizing it was not a safe or healthy situation for the child. With over 10 years in sex work, and no legal way to work in this country, her education and employment options are severely limited. She continues to work in small strip clubs where the owners are willing to look the other way when it comes to her immigration status.

EVE

Another Eastern European immigrant, Eve has been trafficked and re-trafficked for the last 10 year. She currently has three children with three different traffickers, none of which support their children. Her last pimp threw her and her children out on the street after deciding he no longer wanted to be a pimp. With only a high school education and a lengthy arrest record, Eve continues to be preyed upon by traffickers as she struggles to support her children through the only work she has ever known.

WHEN MINORS AGE OUT

Elle was recruited and groomed by a trafficker who posed as a boyfriend at the age of 16. Growing up without her parents, and raised by her grandparents, Elle craved the love and attention this man gave her. After several years of being trafficked across the US by him, her pimp was killed in a violent altercation in the streets of their hometown. Heartbroken, Elle begin searching for love, ending up re-trafficked repeatedly, and sold between pimps. She has been beaten, raped, robbed, and hospitalized all over the country. She has been seen as a nuisance to law enforcement, and ignored by medical professionals. After 16 years, Elle has a felony record, no work experience, and never finished high school. Still longing for love and a family, Elle fell in love with a drug dealer who promised her everything she ever wanted. After having a baby together, this man begin viciously beating her, and telling her that if she continued to prostitute herself to support their family, she needed to begin recruiting younger women to work for him. Terrified for her child's safety, she left him, only to be told by the judge that because he lived in her house, she would have to legally evict him first, and then the judge ordered joint custody of the child.

DREA

At 24, Drea has been in The Game for 8 years, trafficked and exploited by different men who promised to take care of her and help her become successful. In 2014, Drea left The Life and return to school to pursue her dream of working in the medical profession. Sadly, one day a trafficker approached her while waiting at a bus stop on her way to school, and lured her back in.

SHAY

First recruited in high school, Shay escaped her pimp after he murdered her best friend in a fit of rage. With no high school diploma or work experience outside of sex work, Shay continues to work in prostitution, as her parents and siblings depend on her for financial survival.

MARI

First exploited at 17, Mari spent almost eight years in The Game, under the control of her trafficker and the father of her children. She finally succeeded in getting away from him, and continued to work in prostitution to put herself through school. Upon completion of school, Mari has started her own business and her former pimp is now taking her to court to seek joint custody of their children, all the while trying to lure her back into The Life. He refuses to financially support his children because she refuses to be prostituted for his profit.

BRITT

Britt was raised by her grandparents, and never knew her parents. At 15, she was recruited out of high school. She has been trafficked for 10 years now. She has lost three close friends over the past four years, all prostituted women who were murdered by customers. Britt had her first child with her first pimp at the age of 18, and lost custody of the child to her trafficker. She has not seen him in over five years now. Her most recent pimp is the father of her second child. Knowing only The Game and the pimp culture, Britt tried going to college several years ago, but was caught back up and re-trafficked. Extensive trauma and drug use keep Britt from being able to see a world outside the one she is currently trapped in.

KAY

Kay begin talking to a man online when she was 17 that lived across the country. Waiting until she turned 18, he suggested that their relationship was serious and that she should move to live with him. Leaving her family and friends behind, Kay expected to run into the arms of a handsome man in his 30's. Instead, a man in his late 40's picked her up from the airport and took her to his house that he kept three other older women who worked for him. One of the women had just had a child, and it was expected that Kay carry the brunt of the financial responsibilities of the household. She was groomed and trained, and under supervision constantly. After a year, Kay's pimp gave her a car to drive that was in his name, telling her it was a reward for working for him. Two weeks later, she discovered that her pimp had given her an STD, and she tried leaving in the car, only to have her abuser call the police and report his car as stolen. Crushed and discouraged, she returned to his home. Now, two years later (and four years since she first talked to him online), Kay has a child with her trafficker and continues to work under his control while he serves several years of federal time.

DRUG ADDICTION

DIOR

Under the control of a local music artist from the age of 18, Dior spent 7 years being trafficked all over the US, while her pimp used his music business as a front for his criminal activities. Dior left with nothing three years ago. She is currently living with one of her customers, and has made several attempts to exit sex work. Unfortunately, a prescription pain pill addiction and rapidly deteriorating physical health prevent her from being able to move forward.

SNOW

Caught in the world of abusers and illicit substances, Snow has been sexually exploited since she can remember. Her most recent trafficker promised to help her get clean and get her life together, so she desperately devoted two years of her life to him, believing that he was the solution to all of her problems. However, after two years, he suddenly abandoned her, causing a severe relapse that left her near dead. Snow is now emotionally vulnerable, and searching for another savior to help her get clean again.

KEYSHA

A single mother at 17, and first trafficked just before her 18th birthday, Keysha has been in The Game for seven years. She is currently under the control of crack cocaine and methamphetamines, introduced to her by her pimp, and living in a motel with her pimp and daughter on a well-known track. Her daughter must leave the room at any hour of the night for her mother to be sold to customers.

*All names and locations in these case studies have been changed to protect the women's identities.

CASE STUDY EXAMINATION QUESTIONS

1. Is this a case of sex trafficking?

2. What obstacles does the young woman face in finding her freedom?

3. What resources might be available to her?

4. What needs does she have in going through the process of finding her freedom?

5. What support system does she already have in place? How can this be enhanced?

6. What challenges might arise during the process?

7. Do you think that she would be willing to implicate her trafficker in the court of law?

8. What local businesses might be able to contribute to her support system?

CONTACT US

How you can connect with Free Our Girls.

www.freeourgirls.org

www.freeourgirlsblog.org

https://www.facebook.com/FreeOurGirlsInc

www.twitter.com/_FreeOurGirls

Newsletter - http://eepurl.com/bCTMnf

CONTACT US DIRECTLY

info@freeourgirls.org

(888)-539-0645 or (303)621-4269

PO Box 336391, Greeley, CO 80633

SUPPORT US

http://freeourgirls.org/support.html

PayPal - paypal@freeourgirls.org

GoFundMe – www.gofundme.com/m20t5g

ADDITIONAL RESOURCES

Access to the National Education and Support Team online support forum for parents and families of victims and survivors is available with a referral from a local community resource, or you can contact Free Our Girls directly.

If you are in contact with a victim or survivor outside of the state of Colorado, please contact Free Our Girls for her to be connected directly to our survivor-leader and founder through social media!

_____

has successfully completed the *Free Our Girls' Human Trafficking Awareness, Prevention & Response: A Comprehensive Manual*. This book meets the objectives as outlined by the Department of Homeland Security.

Date: _____/_____/_____/

Made in the USA
Monee, IL
23 August 2023

41480100R10040